Properties of Materials

Heavy or Light

Charlotte Guillain

Heinemann Library
Chicago, Illinois

www.heinemannraintree.com
Visit our website to find out
more information about
Heinemann-Raintree books.

To order:
☎ Phone 888-454-2279
▨ Visit www.heinemannraintree.com
to browse our catalog and order online.

Designed by Joanna Hinton-Malivoire
Photo research by Elizabeth Alexander
Printed and bound by South China Printing Company Ltd

13 12 11 10 09
10 9 8 7 6 5 4 3 2 1

Library of Congress Cataloging-in-Publication Data
Guillain, Charlotte.
  Heavy or light / Charlotte Guillain.
    p. cm. -- (Properties of materials)
  Includes bibliographical references and index.
  ISBN 978-1-4329-3287-9 (hc) -- ISBN 978-1-4329-3295-4
(pb) 1. Weight (Physics)--Juvenile literature. 2. Matter--
Properties--Juvenile literature. I. Title.
  QC111.G85 2008
  620.1'129--dc22
                          2008055121

Acknowledgments
The author and publishers are grateful to the following for
permission to reproduce copyright material: Alamy pp. **9**
(© mediablitzimages (UK) Limited), **19** (© Jupiterimages/Creatas);
© Capstone Publishers p. **22** main (Karon Dubke); Getty Images
pp. **8** (Jamie Grill/Iconica), **10** (Betsie Van der Meer/Stone+), **13**,
23 middle (Dorling Kindersley), **17** (Tim Hall/Taxi); Photolibrary
pp. **5** (David Stover/Imagestate), **6** (Jonathan Kirn), **7**, **23** bottom
(Luis Padilla/age footstock), **12**, **23** top (ColorBlind Images/
Blend Images), **14** (Philip Laurell), **18** (© FRUMM John/Hemis);
Shutterstock pp. **4** (© Dainis Derics), **11** (© Hallgerd), **15** (©
Jaimie Duplass), **16** (© mates), **20** (© prism_68), **21** (© Brian A.
Jackson), **22** middle bottom (© anacarol).

Cover photograph of a kite reproduced with permission of
istockphoto (© Piotr Sikora). Back cover photograph of dandelion
seeds reproduced with permission of Shutterstock (© Brian A.
Jackson).

The publishers would like to thank Nancy Harris and Adriana
Scalise for their assistance in the preparation of this book.

Every effort has been made to contact copyright holders of
any material reproduced in this book. Any omissions will
be rectified in subsequent printings if notice is given to the
publisher.

Contents

Heavy Materials

Some things are heavy.

Heavy things are hard to lift.

Heavy things weigh a lot.

Heavy things can be solid.

Light Materials

Some things are light.

Light things are easy to lift.

Light things do not weigh a lot.

Light things can be soft.

Heavy and Light Materials

A metal car is heavy. It is hard to lift.

Metal foil is light. It is easy to lift.

A tree trunk is heavy.

It is hard to lift.

A twig is light.
It is easy to lift.

You can tell if something is heavy or light.

You can feel if something is heavy
or light.

Heavy things are hard to move.

Light things are easy to move.

Sometimes things look heavy.

Sometimes things look light.

Quiz

Which things look heavy?
Which things look light?

Picture Glossary

 **metal** hard, shiny material

 **metal foil** very thin sheets of metal. Foil is often used to wrap food.

 **solid** fixed shape that is not a gas or a liquid

Index

Note to Parents and Teachers
Before Reading
Tell children that some materials are heavy and some are light. Heavy materials are hard to lift and light materials are easy to lift. In partners, ask children to brainstorm a list of heavy and light materials. When they are done, ask the children to share examples and create a chart with one column for heavy objects and one column for light objects.

After Reading
Give children a clipboard, pencil, and piece of paper with two columns—heavy objects and light objects. Tell the children that they are going to go on a hunt around the classroom for heavy and light objects. Put them in small groups. Children can draw or write the objects they see in the appropriate columns. Give them fifteen minutes. When the hunt is done, ask the children the following questions:
1.	What objects did you find?
2.	Which object is the heaviest?
3.	Which object is the lightest?